Real Conversations

Beginning Listening and Speaking Activities

BOOK 2

INSTRUCTOR'S MANUAL

Ruth Larimer
Monterey Institute of International Studies
Monterey, California

Sherry Vaughn
Santa Rita Union School District
Salinas, California

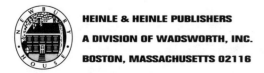

HEINLE & HEINLE PUBLISHERS
A DIVISION OF WADSWORTH, INC.
BOSTON, MASSACHUSETTS 02116

★★

Publisher: Stanley J. Galek
Editorial Director: Christopher Foley
Project Coordinator: Talbot F. Hamlin
Assistant Editor: Erik Gundersen
Editorial Production Manager: Elizabeth Holthaus
Manufacturing Coordinator: Lisa McLaughlin
Text and Cover Design: DECODE, Inc.
Illustrations: Precision Graphics & DECODE, Inc.

02668

Heinle & Heinle Publishers is a division of Wadsworth, Inc.

Manufactured in the United States of America.

ISBN 0-8384-23477

10 9 8 7 6 5 4 3

Contents

An Introduction for the Teacher

Real Conversations is a listening and speaking series for people newly arrived in the United States or other beginning students of English. We hope you will enjoy using *Real Conversations* as much as we enjoyed collecting the authentic data and writing the units.

Both of us had written materials before, but they were materials of the sort where one sits in a room trying to speculate on what native speakers might say and do in some situation. This was a totally different experience. We asked students what they needed to learn about in ESL class and they named several of what we call survival situations. Then we proceeded to tape-record a number of these situations as we traveled throughout the United States and went about our lives at home. We also enlisted friends of various ages and sexes to tape their interactions, since it became clear very early on that language was different between men and women, between children and adults, and to some extent, in different geographical regions. During the collection of data we learned a host of interesting things about the English language, and we realized that our textbooks often mislead students about how English is used.

Real Conversations includes language that occurred frequently in our samples and language from all over the United States. It is true that no conversation sample is really a prototype. Every time a situational variable is changed, some aspect of the conversation will change. But all of our samples happened *somewhere* and were uttered by *someone,* and this is a huge improvement over the inauthentic language invented by the armchair curriculum writer.

In *Real Conversations,* we have made it our policy to avoid editing sentences or conversations. What we have done is to select the simplest versions of conversations or the first parts of longer conversations used in a given situation. For example, one person went into the drug store and said, "Could you possibly tell me where you have the shampoo?" This sentence, for obvious reasons, did not make it into Book 1. On the other hand, more than one person said, "Excuse me. Where are the …?" This provided a starting place for beginning students.

If you are used to teaching units based on a grammatical syllabus, you may find that some lessons are short of new forms while others, especially in Book 2, include some forms that are traditionally thought of as "hard" for beginners. (The present perfect form "Have you had …?" in doctor-patient interaction and employment interviews is an example.) We have made every attempt to sequence the activities so that teaching problems would be minimized (numbers 1-10 before 11-20; numbers up to 100 before money, etc.), but we have refused to sacrifice authenticity in order to teach a form that traditionalists might think "belongs" in a given lesson. At any point where the language seems too "hard," you can use the utterances as chunks to be comprehended in context and analyzed later.

You will notice that question and answer forms appear in most of the lessons. This question and answer discourse is the type of interaction we most often participate in when we are dealing with everyday service encounters. Many times the consumer/student can survive with just short, one-word answers if he or she understands the questions being posed by service employees. Other times the consumer needs to ask the questions. Although the students usually take both roles in the speaking activities, even students who can participate in only the simplest listening activities will learn to recognize new words and the types of questions Americans use.

Although our eventual goal is to help students recognize the information they need from the tangle of natural native speaker speech around them, you will notice that we always begin the Units with vocabulary recognition activities to give students anchor points. In Book 1, these are extensive; in Book 2, the students move more quickly to extracting information from the authentic conversations. The vocabulary activities are ordered so that students are led to recognize and later to use the words without having to overtly "memorize." As they begin to listen to and operate on the full conversations, the structures, too, should become familiar. Again, students will internalize models without drilling.

As a transition to the speaking activities, there is a full presentation of several of the authentic conversations so those who still feel insecure about producing language can "practice," those who are marginally literate can "read along," or those whose intonation is non-native-like can imitate the native speakers' models. We have purposely left the instructions for the "listen and practice the real conversations" activities very general, since the teacher may want to have students do any of the above-mentioned activities—or none at all, leaving the dialogues as reference materials for the students.

The partner practice activities are designed to help the students get the feeling of putting together original utterances closely based on the models (or at least using an authentic model they have learned). We hope the teacher will go to the trouble of carefully setting up the information gap activities so the students get some real practice in communicating, using the new language from the lesson.

The final sections are "Watch Out!" (in some units) and the grammar summaries. "Watch Out!" introduces the student to some of the subtle differences in the way structures or idioms are used in target situations. The grammar summaries are provided for a recap of the forms introduced in the unit. In this instructor's manual we go into some detail about the language of the unit as summarized in these sections.

All the listening activities are recorded on the cassette tapes for *Real Conversations*. Each item is repeated. Pauses are provided between items, but you may wish to pause longer, either turning off the tape player or using its pause button (if it has one). If your player has a digital counter, you may wish to write on the instructions for each activity the number at which the recording of that activity begins. This will make it easier should you wish to repeat the recording for a particular activity. A tapescript is provided in the student text for reference and for practice in situations in which use of the tapes is impossible. (This script does not include all the repeats.)

We hope you will enjoy using *Real Conversations*. We hope it will help you to empower beginning students to understand, and begin to use, some "real conversations" of their own.

Ruth E. Larimer

Sherry Vaughn

Street Directions

This unit is designed to help students ask questions about the location of public buildings around town and to understand the answers.

Competency-related items: asking about community resources underlies various competencies. The map-based activities are a basis for map work of various types.

Setting the scene

Although we have used a map to illustrate this lesson and to provide motivation for direction-asking activities, it is not really a full lesson on map reading (which might involve directions such as N, S, E, W, reading a legend, etc.) It does, however require students to orient themselves in an abstract space, which is difficult for students from some cultures. If this is the students' first map-based lesson, you will need to give them a group orientation to the map. The most concrete way would be to draw "blocks" on the floor and have them pace out instructions. This of course may be impossible in many classrooms. Thus, you may want to start with the illustration.

Instructions for Activities

★1★ Vocabulary

Introductory activities (to be done before using the book)

Put the city picture (page 1), on an overhead transparency and have the students watch while you say things like, *This is a city like* (name a well-known town). *Here are two people talking. One person is a tourist. She is lost. This is the police station* (demonstrate if necessary, with siren noises, for example). *It is on the left* (demonstrate with your back to them). *This is the parking garage. It is on the*

right. The advantage to beginning this way is that the students get an overall picture of the type of vocabulary they will hear and the setting they will be working with. The disadvantage is that they may begin furiously writing down the words. You will need to tell them just to listen first and that they will see all the words in the book.

Activity 1. Listen and look. (pp. 2-3)

Now the students are ready to listen to the individual items carefully and get more familiar with them. Make sure they are all on page 2 and that they are pointing to each item as the tape names it, or put the page on an overhead transparency and point to the appropriate picture as the tape names the items. Go over the items as often as necessary for the students to understand and feel comfortable.

★2★ Listen to Real Conversations

Activity 2A. Listen and circle. (pp. 4-6)

The students will begin to hear place and direction items in the context of short, authentic conversations. They will need to circle the correct place or direction they hear. Put an example on the board.

Say, *Excuse me. Do you know where the post office is?* Say it again and ask the students what you should do, then draw a circle around the post office.

Now begin Activity 2A. The first one is done for them. Have them listen to item one and circle over the dotted line. Then proceed to number 2. You may need to play each item more than once if they are difficult for the students.

Activity 2B. Listen and draw a line. (p. 7)

In this activity, the students will hear a short conversation and they will need to connect the building name to the location by drawing a line, for example:

They hear,

> A: Where's the post office?
> B: Um. It's down this street.

They draw the line.

Turn to page 7. The first line is traced in. Play the tape of the first item and have the students trace the line from the library to the person who says, "I'm sorry, I don't live here."

Now proceed to number 2. Replay the conversation as often as necessary before moving on. Continue with the remaining items. Note that there are more possible "answer" pictures than students will actually use. These "distractors" force students to listen carefully to each conversation. You may need to pause after each conversation, and/or to replay the conversations.

Activity 2C. Listen and write on the map. (p. 8)

This is the first map exercise, and it may be very difficult for students from some cultures. You may want to go back to page 1 and review the directions to the various buildings as a group. Put the picture on an overhead transparency. Say things like:

Example X:

> *Excuse me. Do you know where the post office is?*

They should say:

> *–Yes, it's two blocks up.*

or

> *–Straight ahead.*
> *–Up this street.*

Then put a letter X on the picture of the post office on the overhead. Do a couple of these if it seems difficult. Now have the students open their books to page 8. Play the tape for item 1. Have students write the number 1 next to the question mark by the building "right up the street on the left." If they seem at all confused, you may want to do this activity one item at a time, waiting for everyone to get an answer before writing the correct number on the transparency. If they seem ready to go ahead after number one, do all of the items and then check the answers together and listen to the tape again to verify.

★3★ Practice

Activity 3. Practice the real conversations. (p. 9)

This activity is for those students who cannot move directly from hearing the conversations to using them in communicative ways. It also gives those for whom the written form is an aid, a chance to see the whole conversation in the book.

Have the students listen to the tape and repeat the dialogues, trying to approximate native speaker intonation. You may want to have half the class be "A" and half the class be "B" or have them practice in pairs.

★4★ Partner Practice

Activity 4A. Written conversations. (p. 10)

The students have practiced reading and speaking the conversations. Now they have one more activity to reinforce the types and ordering of the sentences and expressions before doing pair work. For this activity, have them use the cut-out phrases on Sheet A. One communicative way to do the activity is to have two students take a set of strips and figure out who is A and who is B. Another is to hand out one phrase to each of a group of students. Tell them not to show their slip to others, but to memorize the words on it. Then by saying their own parts, students can arrange themselves into conversations.

Activity 4B. Talk to someone. (pp. 10-12)

This is an "information gap" activity. The object of it is to force the students to engage in a real communication, that is, one where the task cannot be accomplished unless they listen to and understand their partner and also make themselves understood. The students will each have a map with different buildings identified (one on page 11 and one on page 12). Have them put a file folder or binder between them so they cannot see each other's map.

Partner A begins by asking for the items listed on page 11 (e.g. the library).

Partner B must look at his or her map, find the library and give directions to A, e.g. "Go up one block. Turn right. It's on the left."

A writes the name "library" on the building at this location.

Partner A can continue to ask for her or his other two items and fill in their names based on B's directions. Then B can ask for the location of his or her three items. When they are finished, they can check maps to see if their locations match.

The teacher and one student should demonstrate this activity before the students begin. You may want to demonstrate several of the conversations as models. It is somewhat difficult to set up information gap pair activities with low level students, but it is well worth the considerable time it will take the first time since you will use this type of activity again and again in this book, and the students will come to enjoy it and see the value of the practice they get.

 Try It Out

Activity 5A. Draw a map. (p. 13)

Draw a map of the neighborhood surrounding the school and put in boxes for the important buildings nearby. The students fill in the building names. If this is difficult and maps are still abstract, tell them to go on a "field trip" around the neighborhood, taking the maps, locating the buildings, and filling them in on the maps one by one.

Next, if possible, go to the chamber of commerce or auto club and get enough maps of the downtown area of the city for each two or three students. Ask them to work together to find and circle their school, the post office, a high school, a library, a church (or whatever is important in their community).

Activity 5B. Go out and ask. (p. 13)

This is the students' chance to try out their new language. Have students go out in pairs and each ask a passerby where a nearby building is. The one who is not asking should write in the directions that the passerby gives. They will not be able to write the whole conversation, but they can note phrases they recognize.

★6★ Grammar summary

There are two grammar structures in this lesson: The "where" question and prepositional phrases. In Book 1 the students learned to ask for directions in stores and public buildings using "where" questions. These are seen as appropriate (i.e. polite enough) for situations where we ask an employee whose job it is to help us. In stores it can also be presumed that there is a good chance that the clerks will have the information being requested. On the street, however, when we approach a stranger for help, we almost never use a direct "where" question; we embed it in a "Do you know?" or (less often) "Can you tell me?" question. In addition to being more polite, the embedded question reflects the possibility that the stranger on the street may be a tourist who is unable to provide the information.

If the question form is discussed, talk about it as a frame that combines "Do you know" and "where the (library, etc.) is?"

Breakfast

This unit presents language used in a typical American situation of breakfast in a restaurant. It includes vocabulary for ordering breakfast items, useful structures for different kinds of requests, and comprehension of offers of service.

Competency items include concepts underlying consumer economics and health and nutrition.

Setting the Scene

Breakfast eaten in a restaurant may be a new concept for some students, and the breakfast bar or buffet style be even more unusual. (We found the "breakfast bar" in family restaurants in places as diverse as California and Massachusetts.) You could start with the picture on page 14 and discuss what the people are doing, what time it might be (anywhere from 7AM to 11AM or 1PM on Sunday is common; if it is between about 10AM and 1PM we may call it "brunch").

Instructions for Activities

 **Vocabulary**

Introductory activities (to be done before using Unit 2 in the book)

Whether you want to begin discussing what the students eat for breakfast or not depends on your judgment of the vocabulary available to them. If it will be difficult for them to produce any description of their own breakfast, it might be better to use vocabulary pictures before discussing breakfast in their cultures.

If you have magazine pictures of breakfast items, such as scrambled eggs, bacon, and English muffins,

you may want to do some response activities before beginning the book. For example, put the pictures along the board or tape to the wall. Name them as you point to them. Then ask the students to point without your example.

Example: Point to the eggs.
Point to the English muffins.
Point to the bacon.
etc.

Now ask yes/no questions. (Do you eat eggs? Do you eat toast?) There will be plenty of new words in the lesson, so it can't hurt to do some of them this way first and lighten up the task of learning all the new vocabulary.

Now proceed to the book.

Activity 1. Listen and look (pp. 15-16)

Ask the students to listen and point to the items in the book as the tape names them, or put the page on the overhead and point as the items are named. Let the students listen as often as necessary.

❷ Listen to Real Conversations

Activity 2A. Listen and circle (p. 17)

This time the students will hear a real conversation and will have to choose and mark the breakfast item or combination of items they hear.

An activity with more than one item in the picture is new for them, so demonstrate on the board by drawing three pictures.

Example:

Read a conversation like,

> A: Can I take your order?
> B: *Yeah; I'd like coffee and toast.*

and ask them which one to circle. When they point to or say "coffee and toast," circle it. If they seem to understand, proceed to item one. This is done for them. Play the tape and ask them to circle over the dotted line. Proceed to the rest of the items. Stop the tape after each item, and replay it if necessary. The combinations get more difficult as the activity continues.

Activity 2B. Read and draw a line (p. 18)

This is one of the few reading activities in "Real Conversations." We felt that it was important to show authentic menu items while discussing restaurant ordering. If students are not literate enough to read the menu, read the items and ask the students to draw the lines. In any case, do one example on the board. You might write and draw:

1. 2 eggs

2. 2 eggs, toast, coffee

3. coffee & toast

Read each one and demonstrate drawing the lines.

Now proceed to the book. It would be very helpful to use an overhead transparency, either to do the activity together or to check answers if the students have done it on their own.

NOTE: Normally you are served water when you sit down in an American restaurant. In some areas of the United States when there are drought conditions, water is not served unless the customers ask for it. Thus the menu says "Water served on request." Customers need to ask for water if they want it.

Activity 2C. Listen and circle "yes" or "no." (pp. 19-20)

In this activity, students will hear a full conversation including several food items. They should read the list of items before hearing the conversation. Then, as they listen to the conversation, they circle the "yes" beside the item if it is mentioned and "no" if the item is not mentioned. You should put one example on the board since this is a new type of activity in this book.

Example:

Write:	coffee	yes	no
	water	yes	no
	eggs	yes	no

Say: Hi. What can I get for you?
Uh, Just coffee and a glass of water.
Okay.

Then ask the students which to circle, and demonstrate circling the first two "yes" after coffee and water and the "no" after "eggs." Now proceed to the book and do the first one together. It is done in the book and students should circle over the dotted lines.

★3★ Practice

Activity 3A. Practice the real conversations. (pp. 21-22)

As in the previous unit, this set of conversations can be used as is most useful for the students. They can listen and repeat for fluency or pronunciation, perform in pairs, read along with the tape for reading practice, or just use the dialogues for reference.

Activity 3B. Listen and answer. (p. 23)

This activity can be used either for speaking practice or as a "listen and write" exercise. If the students are literate enough to attempt individual answers, have them listen to each prompt and write down their own response. Then you can go back and repeat the prompt and ask several students to share their responses. For example (item 1), they might generate things like:

"I'd like *coffee, orange juice, milk, etc.*"
   (more polite)
or "I want *coffee, orange juice, etc.* please"
   (less polite)

If they cannot write a response, just play the item on the tape and ask several students to respond orally. You could write responses on the board to help them see the sound-symbol correspondence.

★4★ Partner Practice

Activity 4A. Written conversations (p. 24)

As in Unit 1, have the students cut up the conversation strips (Sheet B) and distribute sets either to pairs or to groups of individuals and have them reconstruct the conversations. Discuss which are appropriate.

Activity 4B. Talk to someone. (p. 24)

This is an information gap conversation activity. The students are to take the roles of waitperson* and customer. The waitperson has a chart and the cut-out pictures on Sheet C for food. B sits at the table and A comes up and hands B the menu (text page 18). A offers food or drink (see Chart A for example sentences). B either says she/he is not ready or orders food. A chooses the correct food pictures and hands them to B. B either accepts them as correct ("Thank you") or corrects the order.

Since this is a new activity type, you should demonstrate how it works by performing it with one student first, where the student is the customer and you are the waiter.

★5★ Try It Out

Activity 5. (p. 25)

For a homework activity, have the students go to one or two restaurants that serve breakfast and look at the menu posted outside (or if you have collected

several menus, you could do this activity in class). The student looks at the menu, chooses a breakfast, and writes down the name of the restaurant, the food items, and the price. This could be expanded to be a lesson in addition if they are told to choose two or more items and add up the prices, reporting the total.

★6★ Watch Out! ✳

There are certain rules of politeness in American English that we don't usually find in grammar books, but that we discover in looking at authentic conversations. For example, if the waitperson offers you food or drinks you can accept by saying "I'd like..." or "I'll have..." These phrases are often used for ordering in fast food restaurants as well (see Book 1, Unit 6). On the other hand, if you call and ask for something extra, even if you would expect to have it (like cream to go with coffee or a fork to eat with), you are not responding to a direct offer and you use the more polite forms "Can I have...?" "Could I have...." or "May I have...." These are accompanied by polite, requesting intonation. (Of course some people will choose to be more demanding and say something like "Waitress, I don't have a fork!" but most of the people in our data used "can," "could," or "may.")

Note also that in traditional grammar books we are told that "May I" is the correct request form while "Can I" is improper. This distinction is being lost in American conversational English, and the use of polite intonation with "Can I" or "Could I" seems to be replacing "May I" in many situations.

★7★ Grammar Summary

There are two offer forms that the students need to understand in this unit. One is a formulaic form the waitperson uses after the customers have looked at the menu: "Are you ready to order?" The other, also used by the waitperson, is an offer to take the order or an offer of specific drinks or food using "Would you like...?" This offer form is useful to students since it is also appropriate for them to use

---

* Although we have traditionally called restaurant servers "waiter" (male) and "waitress" (female), many newspapers and employers have switched over to a non-gender-related term "waitperson" for both males and females (see authentic newspaper ads, text page 57).

when offering food or drinks at home or to a friend in a restaurant.

The main grammatical forms here are orders and request forms. First are the phrases "I'd like" and "I'll have" for *responding* to the waitperson's offer. Although the fully expanded forms "I *would* like…" and "I will have…" were never used in our samples, they *could* occur, and some students will probably appreciate having an explanation of where the contractions came from, structurally.

They will also want to know why people use three different forms in requesting extra items (see "Watch Out!" section for explanation of social usage). *We do NOT advise teaching these request forms as versions of the affirmative ("I can" "I could") with subject-verb inversion.* In the affirmative form the preferred meaning of the modals denotes ability or permission and thus is quite different from the function of polite request in the question forms. We would simply explain that these modals have several different meanings in English, and in this case they are used for polite requests.

Making an Application

In this unit students will work on understanding and responding appropriately to requests for personal information. They will practice orally spelling their names and street names. They will need to understand requests to repeat, spell, and clarify. Students will be introduced to applications and will practice filling out applications, providing their own background information.

Competency-related items in this unit include personal identification information.

Setting the Scene

Many of the language samples in this unit came from employment or employment training interviews. However the information will aid learners in a variety of situations in which personal information is requested such as doctor's office, social security office, and customs or immigration office.

Instructions for Activities

 **Vocabulary**

Introductory activities (to be done before using Unit 3 in the book)

Before students begin this activity, you may want to explain and give examples of full names in the United States and how they are divided into first names, middle names, and last names. Also give examples of initials. You may want to point out that although some applications ask for the first name to be written first, many ask for the last name first.

Activity 1. Listen and look. (p. 28)

In the lesson, students will listen to the tape and look at the application. Students should point to

each item (name, address, phone, etc.) as they hear it. Let them listen several times if needed. You will probably need to explain some of the items in greater detail and give examples.

After students seem to understand the vocabulary on the application, it would be good practice for them to fill out this application with their own personal information. You will then have an opportunity to check for understanding and give further explanation when needed.

② Listen to Real Conversations

Activity 2A. Listen and circle. (p.29)

It would be a good idea to review the letters of the alphabet before doing this activity. You may want to bring in a chart with the letters of the alphabet on it as well as 5" x 8" cards, each with one letter of the alphabet written on it. The chart can be used for review of the alphabet and can be referred to for practice throughout the unit. Place it so that all students can see it and can refer to it at any time. The cards can be used to help students compare and contrast various letters that they find difficult, such as the vowels and the consonants "B" and "V," "C," "S," and "Z," and "G" and "J." Students can hold up the cards containing the letters being worked on and stand in different locations in the classroom. Call out one of the letters and have the class point to that letter. This can be repeated with few or several letters at a time until the students are quite certain of the letters.

In the activity, one item (name, address, phone number, date, etc.) from each conversation is printed on the page in the correct form and two incorrect forms. Students will listen to short conversations. As students listen to each conversation, they will look at the three items and circle the correct one. Play the first conversation. The students should trace the circle around the correct item in number 1. Continue to work through the activity. You may need to replay the tape one or more times.

Activity 2B, 2C. Listen and draw a line. (pp. 30-31)

In this activity students will be looking at completed applications. They will be listening to excerpts from employment interviews in which the interviewer is asking for or verifying information on an application, and they will be drawing a line to the section of the application that is being discussed. Before beginning the actual activity, you should go over the two applications with students and help them to become familiar with all the vocabulary and information that is included. It would be ideal to use an overhead projector to go over the two applications.

When students are sufficiently familiar with the two applications, move to number 1, the example, in the book. Play the tape and have the students trace the line to the "Birth date" section of the first application, as that is the information being requested. Move on when students are ready to complete the activity. You may want to play each excerpt two or more times before going on to the next.

Activity 2D. Listen and write. (p. 32)

In this activity students will hear only requests for information. After each request they should write the appropriate information about themselves. Each request is recorded twice, but you may wish to play it again. Then pause the tape so that students have enough time to fill in the information. Because each student will have different information, you will need to spend enough time going over the finished activity to ensure that the questions were understood by all.

★3★ Practice

Activity 3. Listen and practice the real conversations. (pp. 33-36)

Students will be listening to long sections of interviews in this activity. They will be able to get the overall feeling of an interview. They should not memorize, and probably not even repeat these conversations, as they include many repetitions and false starts.

You may want to begin the activity while the students' books are closed. Divide the class into five groups. Have one group listen for and write the name of the applicant, one group write the address, one group the birth date, one the social security number, and one the languages spoken. *Because of their length, each interview is recorded once only.* You should play the first interview two or more times while students focus on the one piece of information they are to listen for. Discuss, and perhaps write the results on the board or overhead. Then have students open their books and follow the conversations as they hear them. Check the information the students wrote. Discuss any unfamiliar vocabulary.

Play the second interview and let students read the conversation as they listen to it. Discuss unfamiliar vocabulary, but reassure students that they do not need to understand each word to understand what information is being requested of the applicant.

Expansion Activity

Because the authentic language in Units 3, 4, and 5 is rather varied and thus more difficult to use in partner practice, you may want to skip ahead to the activities suggested in the teacher's instructions for the grammar summary. This will help the students gain command of a limited number of the structures used by the interviewer for use in their partner activities. The rest can be left for comprehension only.

★4★ Partner Practice

Activity 4A. Written conversations. (p. 37)

Students will use the cut-out sentences on Sheets D and E. They should work in pairs. They will put the strips in the correct order to make conversations. They can act out the conversations with their partners. Volunteers can act out the conversations for the class. Another way you may want to do this activity is to give one cut-out sentence to each of a group of students and have them arrange themselves in order.

Activity 4B. Talk to someone. (p. 37)

This is an information gap activity. Students fill out the application on page 38, providing their own personal information. They should leave two or three items blank. Then the students work in pairs. They trade applications. One partner is the interviewer who verifies the information and spellings on the application. The interviewer also must ask for and fill in the information of the items that have been left blank. Partners change roles. When partners have played each role they check the information that has been added by their partner.

⑤ Watch Out!

You will want to explain to students that the "do" and "did" questions are used when someone is requesting new information. When people are merely verifying information that they already have they are more likely to use tag questions ending in "... right?"

There is another very common type of "question" found in these conversations, a fragment or statement that is used as a request for information or verification. You may want to explain to your students that often we request information without using a standard question form. There are numerous examples of this in the conversations, for example, "And your phone number?" "Okay, date of birth," "Your name please," and "Uhkay, now you have your associate's degree in business administration?" You may want to have your students look for other examples in the conversations so that they are aware of how common this requesting technique is.

⑥ Grammar Summary

The conversations in this unit include question/answer interactions. There are five basic question forms, three of which occur more than once:

1. *What is* your address?
          your phone number?
          your social security number?
2. *Do you* have a driver's license?
          have a middle initial?
          speak any language other than _____?
3. (fragments) And the last name?
          And your social security number?
          And your phone number?

Four other types of questions occur once and should probably be left alone structurally and only used as a context for comprehension of the content.

1. Did you...?
2. Who referred you?
3. How did your _____ hear about this?
4. Now you have your degree in business administration?

The "what" and "do" questions, which occur more frequently, could be highlighted, perhaps including the "did" question to show present and past tenses.

You could put a frame on the board and ask the students to generate some questions an interviewer might ask, for example,

      Do you have _____ ?

They may need to practice several possible items in this frame so they will have command of them when they do the partner practice activities.

Do the same thing with the form,

      What is your _____ ?

This will give the students command of two of the possible questions to use.

At the Doctor's Office

This unit is designed to introduce students to the language they will need to use and understand to participate in a health care situation. Students will need to understand requests for health information and to describe symptoms of illness.

The competency items in this unit relate to solving health problems.

Note that this unit, and Units 5 and 6, include a different style of illustration from that used in earlier units. The cartoon style was chosen because of its capacity to convey feelings, actions, occupations, and such abstractions as styles of music with greater clarity and immediacy than either realistic drawings or photographs. Illustrator Arnie Levin's work appears regularly in *The New Yorker* and other publications.

Setting the Scene

Although a doctor's office is probably a familiar setting to most students, you may want to look at and discuss the picture on page 40 with the class before beginning the unit.

Instructions for Activities

 **Vocabulary**

Activity 1. Listen and look. (p. 41)

Play the tape and have students look at and point to the appropriate pictures as they listen to the vocabulary words. Some further teacher explanation may be needed.

❷ **Listen to Real Conversations**

Activity 2A. Listen and circle. (pp. 42-43)

In this activity students will listen to questions about various symptoms. As they listen to each

question they will look at three pictures and circle the one that corresponds to the symptom that is mentioned in the question. Let the students hear the first question. They should trace the circle around the correct symptom (ear ache). Play the tape for the rest of the activity. You may want to pause after each item and/or to replay the tape one or more times.

Activity 2B. Listen and draw a line. (p. 44)

Students will listen to excerpts from doctor/patient conversations in this activity, each of which is dealing with a particular symptom. They will draw a line from the number of the excerpt (two line dialogue) to the picture of the symptom that is being discussed. Play the tape for number one and have the students trace over the line to the correct answer. Move on when students are ready to complete the activity while listening to the tape. You may want to pause the tape after each dialogue and let the students hear the tape at least one more time.

Activity 2C. Listen and check "yes," "no," or "I don't know." (pp. 45-46)

In this activity students will be listening to longer conversations in which more than one symptom is discussed. Students will listen to each conversation to determine whether or not the patient has the symptoms being discussed. For each conversation there are four symptoms listed in the book. The students will check the "yes" box if the patient does have the symptom, the "no" box if the patient does not have the symptom. If the symptom is not discussed in the conversation, the student will check the "I don't know" box. Play the tape of the first conversation. The students will listen as they look at the activity in their book. Number one is done for them. You probably will want to discuss the answers and replay the first conversation before moving on to the other conversations. Replay the tape as often as needed.

★★★

❸ Practice

Activity 3. Practice the real conversations. (pp. 47-48)

Have the students listen to the tape and repeat the conversations, trying to approximate native speaker intonation. You may want to have them practice in pairs.

❹ Partner Practice

Activity 4A. Written conversations. (p. 49)

Use the cut-out sentences on Sheet F and G. Students can work in pairs and put the sentences in a logical order to make conversations. They can act out the conversations with their partners. Volunteers can act out the conversations for the class. You may prefer to give one sentence strip to each of the group of students and have the students arrange themselves in a logical order. Then they should read the conversation in the order they have arranged to check that the conversation makes sense. There are various ways that the sentence strips can be ordered; any order that makes sense is correct.

Expansion Activity

Because the authentic language is this unit is rather varied and thus more difficult to use in partner practice, you may want to skip ahead to the activities suggested in the grammar summary. This will help the students gain command of a limited number of the structures used by the interviewer for use in their partner activities. The rest can be left for comprehension only.

Activity 4B. Talk to someone. (pp. 49-50)

The goal of this information gap activity is for one student, the "doctor," to discover the symptoms of another student, the "patient." To begin this activity, write the names of the symptoms the students have studied on the board or overhead (cough, chills, diarrhea, etc.). Ask the students to pretend they are sick, and have each student choose three symptoms. They will write their three symptoms in the box on

page 49 or on a 3" x 5" card or piece of paper. They should not show what they have written to their classmates.

After writing their "symptoms," students should turn to the chart on page 50. They will divide into pairs and write their partner's name in the first space next to the word "names" at the top of their chart. (See example at the bottom of page 49.) They will then begin the role playing. Partner A is the "doctor" and Partner B is the "patient." They will hold a conversation in which the "doctor" will find out the symptoms of the "patient's" illness. The doctor will ask questions of the patient such as "Have you had a fever?" The patient will look at his list of three symptoms and answer "yes" or "no." (The patient may also volunteer further information such as "no, I've had a stomach ache.") The doctor will then make a check beside the three symptoms that the patient has under the patient's name on the chart. Students will then trade roles.

When both of the partners have played both roles, they will find new partners, write their new partner's names in the next space at the top of the chart and repeat the role-playing activity.

❺ Grammar Summary

The main structures used in the symptom-reporting phase of the doctor's office interactions are the present perfect and the present perfect progressive. If you are used to working from a grammatical syllabus, you may be shocked that these structures appear in a beginning book. Many of us have had significant troubles teaching use and formation of the present perfect to students at much higher levels. One approach to dealing with this is to have the students practice, memorize, or just recognize the forms, since they are really only needed for comprehension. However, most students like to understand structures. Thus, if possible, we recommend that you try some basic explanation. Don't try to explain the overall structure of perfectives in all their forms, but rather take only the structures that appear in the real conversations, one at a time, and help the students generate many examples of the given pattern. For example, you might ask them, *How does the doctor ask about your sickness?* and put a frame such as the following on the board: "Have you had _____ (+noun)?" Then add all the symptoms that can fit into this pattern:

> Have you had an earache?
>   a fever?
>   a sore throat, etc., etc.

Then do the same thing with the pattern: "Have you been _____ (+verb in -ing form)?"

> Have you been vomiting?
>   feeling dizzy?
>   coughing?

If the students are structurally sophisticated enough to ask how this is different from "Do you have…?" (which the doctor also occasionally uses) or "Did you have…?" you might want to draw a time line indicating an action originating in the past and continuing up to the present to show that the doctor is not asking just about past or present but about something that began in the past and is still continuing.

Then you could do the same thing with the answers:

"I've had _____ ." and generate symptoms. (You could also do "I've been _____ (+verb)" but these forms don't happen to occur in the conversations we included.) If the students can maintain attention, and if they are of an age where they are interested in discussing their children's symptoms, you could do the same exercise with, "Has she/he had _____ ?" but this has already become a fairly heavy grammar lesson for a listening book! Remember, the point of the lesson is to understand the doctor and give a comprehensible answer, not to practice certain grammatical forms for accuracy. The students will probably not attain accuracy in present perfect forms at this point.

All in all, this is a complex lesson structurally, but one that students are usually highly motivated to work at. We found it interesting that real doctors used some very different language from what textbooks usually tell us!

The Job Interview

In this unit students will be introduced to various types of jobs and the skills and duties that are related to each job. Students will work on understanding job descriptions and describing their own work-related experience. They will also be introduced to the idea of "selling themselves" to a prospective employer, and how this is considered appropriate and even necessary in the United States.

Competency-related items in this unit include occupational knowledge.

Setting the Scene

Students will learn about types of jobs and job experience and the language of employment interviews, but the primary goal of this unit is to enable students to make a positive presentation in a job interview situation.

Instructions for Activities

 Vocabulary

Activity 1. Listen and look. (pp. 53-54)

This activity introduces students to categories of work as well as specific jobs and tasks. Have students look and point to the appropriate pictures as they listen to the tape. You will probably want to play the tape more than one time and further explain and/or demonstrate any vocabulary that the students find difficult.

 Listen to Real Conversations

Activity 2A. Listen and circle. (p. 55)

Students will hear short interview conversations. As they listen to each conversation, they will look at the four pictures and circle the two that represent jobs that are mentioned in the conversations. Let the students hear the first conversation. They should trace the circles around the two types of work that are mentioned, restaurant work and machine shop work (or machinist). Tell students that the wording in the conversations may not be exactly the same as in the vocabulary, but they should try to listen to get the key words or phrases so that they can understand the gist of the conversation, even though they may not understand all the words. (Notice that in conversations 3 and 5, the words on pages 53 and 54 used in naming the pictures that students now have to circle are not exactly the same as the words they hear on the tape.)

Play the tape for the rest of the activity. You will probably want to pause the tape after each conversation and replay the individual conversations as often as needed before going on.

Activity 2B. Read and draw a line. (pp. 56-57)

This activity will introduce students to classified employment ads. It is not a listening activity, but includes much vocabulary that is important for students who will be in a job interview situation. As classified ads are such a valuable resource for employment seekers, an activity that introduces students to classified ads seems a necessity in a unit on employment.

Students will look at each ad and draw lines to the jobs that are described. The first is done for them. Each ad is illustrated by from one to four pictures, depending on the job or jobs described. You will probably want to read the ads aloud to the class and explain any unfamiliar vocabulary before they begin the activity. Students can work alone, in pairs, or in small groups to complete the activity.

If possible, bring in or ask the students to bring in the classified section of a local newspaper so that they can become more familiar with employment ads. You may want them to find jobs that fit the categories of employment they are studying in this unit, or jobs that interest them. In a later activity they will again be using classified ads, so you may want to save the newspapers that are brought in.

Activity 2C. Listen and circle "yes" or "no." (p. 58)

Students will listen to interview conversations that deal with an applicant's work experience or with the duties of a particular job. In either case, various tasks are mentioned. Students will listen to the conversations while they look at the activity on page 58. They will circle "yes" if the job or experience includes the tasks that are written for each conversation, and "no" if the job or experience does not include the task. Replay the conversations as needed.

★3★ Practice

Activity 3A. Practice the real conversations. (pp. 59-60)

Let the students listen to the conversations on the tape and have them repeat the conversations, trying to approximate native speaker intonation. It might benefit students to practice the conversations with a partner.

Activity 3B. Listen and answer. (p. 61)

In this activity students will hear requests for information. They will respond with information about themselves. Students who are literate may write the appropriate information about themselves on the lines provided. They should not be concerned about writing correctly, as this is primarily an activity to help students understand and respond to typical interview questions. If students are not able to write the answers, have them work in pairs. After each question on the tape, have one student respond to his/her partner. The partner will "check" the response and ask for clarification if necessary. Partners will then trade roles.

Whether the activity has been done individually or in pairs, you will need to spend enough time going over the completed activity and discussing the different answers to ensure that the questions were understood by all.

★4★ Partner Practice

Activity 4A. Written conversations. (p. 62)

Students will use the cut-out sentences on Sheet H. With a partner, they will put the strips in a logical order to make conversations. Partners can act out the conversations, and/or volunteers can act them out for the class. You may prefer to give one sentence to each of a group of students and have them arrange themselves in order.

Expansion Activity.

Because the authentic language in this unit is rather varied and thus more difficult to use in partner practice, you may want to skip ahead to the activities suggested in the grammar summary. This will help the students have command of a limited number of the structures used by the interviewer for use in their partner activities. The rest can be left for comprehension only.

Activity 4B. Talk to someone. (pp. 62-63)

In this activity students will work in pairs. Partner A is the interviewer, and Partner B is the applicant. Partner A will use Form 1 on page 63 and will need to gather enough information from Partner B to fill out the form. Partner A can use the sample questions on page 63 if necessary.

The students will then change roles and Partner B, the "interviewer" will inform Partner A, the "applicant" that the job that is open is in maintenance. Partner B will use Form 2 on page 63 and will gather the information from Partner A to fill out the form. If students have no specific background in maintenance, they will have to use related relevant experience to answer the questions. (See "Try It Out" in the teacher's instructions below.) Demonstrate this activity with one student before having the class do it.

★5★ Try It Out

Activity 5. (p. 64)

This activity again deals with classified employment ads. If you saved the newspapers from Activity

2B, you may use them now. You may prefer to have students get their own newspapers. Students will look through the classified ads and find a job that interests them. Then have them fill out the chart on page 64.

This is a good time to discuss the idea that everyone has some work experience, even if unpaid, and that everyone has some marketable skills. If students have little or no paid work experience, or no work experience in the United States, they may feel that they cannot claim any experience. You may want them to look through the interview conversations in this unit and underline or write down all the positive things that the applicants say about themselves and their experience. It might then be a good idea to have students make a list of all that they can do and of all the positive qualities they have that might be important in a job.

You may want to have them brainstorm all the work or tasks that they have done at any time in their lives. You might then ask for one or more volunteers to list some of these tasks for the class. Discuss how these can relate to employment experience. Cooking, housekeeping chores, painting, and gardening are all work experience. Being reliable, liking to be with people, having good math skills, or being bilingual are all marketable qualities or skills. In many cultures it is inappropriate to bring up one's own good qualities, whereas in the United States it is both appropriate and necessary in order to compete for a job. In our culture this is not considered bragging.

★6★ Watch Out!

Stress to students that in order to make a good impression at a job interview in the United States they must be positive. They must focus on what they can do, and never on what they cannot do. This can be extremely difficult for students from many cultures.

Students also need to understand that in employment interviews it is the responsibility of the applicants to show how their background and experience make them right for the job.

★7★ Grammar Summary

In employment interviews, as in the doctor's office, the present perfect is used frequently by the interviewer to solicit the applicant's general background (all the experience from the past up to the present).

You will have to use judgment here as to how much grammatical discussion the students can tolerate at this point as opposed to a more basic focus on the job titles and descriptions and on understanding the gist of the conversations. If the students are very low level, focus on comprehension and one or two basic past tense answers.

If you want to get into grammar explanation, you could generate a pattern using this form as in the previous lesson, by announcing that you will discuss how the interviewer asks about your experience:

Have you _____ ?
　　　　ever worked?
　　　　worked in maintenance?
　　　　worked in a factory?
What kind of work have you done?

The answer to this sort of question is a listing of job experiences or a description of the jobs that relate to the general topic the interviewer mentions:

I've had experience in schools.
I've had two factory jobs.

(To confuse the issue, interviewees sometimes convert this question to a list of specific experiences stated in the simple past tense, but we would suggest keeping any explanation as simple as possible at this point.)

The general solicit using present perfect can be contrasted with questions about exact times in the past or specific job experience listed on the application, where the interviewer uses simple past tense to refer to a certain job and time:

Okay, in 1990…what did you do?
What did you do at the hotel?

These questions can be answered with simple past tense questions such as:

I was a housekeeper.
I worked in the office.

Making Plans: Movies and Dancing

In this unit, the students will work with days of the week and will review times, prices, and street addresses in a different context from previous units. They will also be introduced to cultural information about types of American popular music and other entertainment, such as nightclubs and movies. The listening activities focus on understanding tapes of theater information and phone conversations about nightclubs. Conversations involve discussion of plans and preferences.

Competency-related items: overview of times, places, and prices, which underlie skills in consumer economics and community services.

Setting the Scene

By this time, students may be able to participate in a simple discussion of their preferred entertainment. You could bring a few magazine pictures of people dancing, watching a movie or listening to music (or use the illustration on page 66). Ask students simple questions like, "What do you like to do?" They can answer "dance," "listen to music," etc. If the students have some working vocabulary, you could go on to "What is your favorite movie?" or "Where do you go dancing?" If that is too difficult, proceed from the picture to the vocabulary page.

Instructions for Activities

 **Vocabulary**

Activity 1. Listen and look. (p. 67)

This activity introduces students to types of entertainment including different types of music and to other terms heard in cinema information tapes and calls to nightclubs. Play the tape and have the students point to the words or pictures. The brief music samples are included as quick auditory "definitions" of the four music types. Play the tape as often as necessary until they understand the terms and concepts. The calendar on page 67 is used only to introduce the days of the week. Days of the month do not occur in the authentic conversations or in the vocabulary list on the tape, but you may want to do some work with days of the month (dates) as an expansion activity. You may also want to discuss the concept of "weekend," which does not occur in the vocabulary but does come up in the real conversations. (Notice that we normally refer to Saturday and Sunday as the weekend when we discuss it out of context, but when we are talking about weekend nights in the context of nightclubs or movies, we mean Friday and Saturday.) An additional idea for expansion would be to spend some time listening to various types of music and identifying which type it is. (This could also be done to expand Activity 2A.) You may want to call attention to the fact that on American calendars, the week starts with Sunday. On calendars used in many other countries, the week is shown as beginning with Monday.

★2★ Listen to Real Conversations

Activity 2A. Listen and circle. (p. 68)

Students will hear segments of conversations between a customer and a nightclub employee. They should look at the three pictures of types of music and circle the one mentioned in the conversation. This is another place where types of music provides a topic for more expansion and discussion of cultural differences and similarities. (E.g. "What kind of music do people like in your native country?")

★★★

Activity 2B. Listen and circle. (p. 69)

In this activity, students will hear segments from cinema information tapes. They should listen for the days of the week and circle those that they hear mentioned. There may be more than one day mentioned.

Activity 2C. Listen and write the prices. (p. 69)

Here, the students will hear a different segment of the movie information recordings, and they will need to write the prices of admission for each kind of customer (general or adults, children, senior citizens). There will be more than one item to write out for each conversation, so you will probably need to replay the tape for the students.

Activity 2D. Listen and write the time (or day). (p. 70)

In this activity, again, the students will hear conversation segments, and they will fill in a blank. This time, however, they will write a time or a day. Items one to three require only one response, but the later ones require the writing of three items per conversation, so the students will probably need to hear the tape more than once.

Activity 2E. Listen and write the address. (p. 71)

Now students listen to yet another segment of the movie tapes and they have a more challenging task: writing out the address given on the tape. Because this may be quite difficult for semi-literate students, the city and street names are given in the box at the top of the page and can be located and copied. Call attention to these before playing the tape.

Activity 2F. Listen and fill in the chart (movies). (p. 72)

This activity is similar to Activity 2D in that students fill in movie times. However, they are now given a larger segment of the conversation and need to listen more carefully for the times. They are also using a chart here instead of simple blanks with contextual cues. Chart reading itself is a skill that is useful for many activities. You may need to explain how the chart works and go over the first item before you play the tape, even though it is done for them in the book.

Activity 2G. Listen and fill in the chart (night clubs). (p.72)

This activity also provides experience with chart completion and may need explanation, since it is a different task from filling in blanks. The conversations are also longer and cover several types of information which students were previously given in short separate segments. They may need help with the first one and/or several repetitions of the tape.

⟨3⟩ Practice

Practice the real conversations. (pp. 73-74)

Have the students practice saying the whole conversations, attempting to replicate the native speaker intonation. Depending on how much practice they need before doing partner practice activities, you may want them to practice saying or performing the conversations in pairs.

⟨4⟩ Partner Practice

Activity 4A. Written conversations. (p. 75)

Students use the sentence cut-outs on sheets I and J to make conversations. They can do this in pairs or in groups so that each individual has one strip and they arrange themselves to make a conversation.

Activity 4B. Talk to someone. (pp. 75-76)

For this activity, students will circulate around the class and ask other students what kind of music they like and fill in the chart on page 76 to document the preferences of the class. When they are finished, they should have documented a number of students' preferences. You can make a rule that they need to do three people or ten people or the whole class, depending on how much time you want to spend on the activity. There are pictures on the chart indicating rock and roll, country, blues, and top 40, but you may want to add some others such as reggae, salsa, or classical, depending on the nature of the class. Individual students may also volunteer music types not on the chart.

You will need to demonstrate this activity, using the first column on the chart. Ask the class to watch while you go up to a student and (if you think they don't know each other's names), ask, *What's your name?* and write the name in the first column of the chart. Then ask, *What kind of music do you like?* When the student answers, put a check in the column under his/her name beside the type of music named. If the students don't understand yet, do another one. Then let them circulate and ask each other.

You might want to tally up the responses and use the results for a basic graphing activity.

★5★ Try It Out

Activity 5. (p. 77)

These activities are intended for homework. If the students are very inexperienced with phone directories, photocopy the appropriate pages and bring them to class. Help them fill out the first column with the name of the theater and phone number. It is best to divide the class up so that a few students call each theater. Then they can compare notes on what they found out about the times and prices and report back to the whole group.

The nightclub call can be handled the same way, except that it is not advisable to have a large number of people calling the same club. Perhaps if there are not enough clubs for everyone to "have his own," the boxes could be divided up so someone asks about dancing, someone about music, and someone else about time or cover charge. Or certain students can be designated to do the calls.

★6★ Grammar Summary

This unit provides practice with three types of "Do you have...?" questions which were seen previously in Units three and four of Book 2. In Book 1, students asked "Do you have the time?"

(Unit 3) and also, "Do you have change?" (Unit 4). In this unit, they also use the new questions with "What kind" and "What time." Since there are only one or two examples of these questions, we suggest that they be taught as chunks; that is, the students should practice asking, "What kind of music do you have?" and "What time do you open?" in their entirety rather than analyzing the grammar.